A Boy Named Jonathan

Jonathan

A True Story of Kindness

Mary Demoff

WestBow Press books may be ordered through booksellers or by contacting:

WestBow Press
A Division of Thomas Nelson & Zondervan
1663 Liberty Drive
Bloomington, IN 47403
www.westbowpress.com
844-714-3454

International Children's Bible®. Copyright© 2015 by Tommy
Nelson, a division of Thomas Nelson, Inc.

ISBN: 978-1-6642-9854-5 (sc)
ISBN: 978-1-6642-9855-2 (hc)
ISBN: 978-1-6642-9853-8 (e)

Library of Congress Control Number: 2023908106

Print information available on the last page.

WestBow Press rev. date: 08/18/2023

WESTBOW
PRESS®
A DIVISION OF THOMAS NELSON
& ZONDERVAN

DEDICATION

To My Husband

You're my hero and best friend! You've supported me wholeheartedly, encouraged me endlessly, and loved me unconditionally! Thank you from the bottom of my heart! And you undoubtedly earned the title of Jonathan's *favorite uncle!*

To Bernie and Debbie (Jonathan's parents)

Your three precious sons are now healed and safely home with Jesus. You persevered faithfully and trusted God completely through the journey. Your love for God and for your boys is profoundly inspiring. Thank you for brightening their world and ours!

To Amy, Christa, Bill, Linda, and Maegan

Your input and dedication to this project means more to me than words can express. Thank you for sprinkling sparkles of kindness into my life!

There once was a boy named Jonathan who was extraordinary. He never *felt* very extraordinary. He never *said* he was extraordinary...but everyone **knew** he was extraordinary. His story begins like this...

Snuggled tight in his mommy's arms, he was as happy as he could be. His mommy and daddy were over the moon excited when he arrived. His mommy's eyes filled with happy tears, and she felt as if her heart could burst with love. ***GIGGLE. GIGGLE. SNIFF. SNIFF.*** *"He's perfect!"* she exclaimed. As they looked into his beautiful blue eyes, his daddy whispered, "We love you, Jonathan!"

After Jonathan celebrated his third birthday, his parents and doctors realized he wouldn't grow up *exactly* like other boys and girls. Although he could do many things other kids could do—like laugh and jump and play—the doctors said there would be some things he would never be able to do. But his parents knew...***he was still perfect!*** God created Jonathan—and you and me—beautifully unique! He made you wonderfully and marvelously. You are exceptional and amazing!

Even though Jonathan would never be able to read a book, drive a car, or even tie his own shoes, our Heavenly Father had an incredible plan for him. Jesus' kindness would shine through Jonathan's life. He would be a world-brightener!

When you meet someone who is different than you, it's the perfect time to make a new friend! You might have the same favorite ice cream. Or you both might love puppies!

NORTH
AMERICA

EUROPE

ATLANTIC
OCEAN

AFRICA

SOUTH
AMERICA

BOTSWANA

ANTARCTICA

ZOOM! ZOOM! Jonathan felt happy riding his bike. And he felt happy playing at the park. But he felt *happiest* telling people how much Jesus loved them! He *loved* to talk about the heroes of the Bible. And he *loved* to talk about heaven. "The Bible says heaven is an *AMAZING* place! No one will ever get sick or feel sad! Everyone will be happy! Do **you** want to go to heaven?" he would ask. When Jonathan talked about Jesus, *people stopped and listened!*

He also loved adventure! *WHOOOSH! WHEEEEE!* He loved roller coasters, playground slides, and airplane rides! One exciting day, his dad announced, "Pack your suitcase! We're going on a mission trip!"

"YIPPEE!" exclaimed Jonathan. After a **very long** plane ride...his family arrived in Botswana, Africa. He met people who were lonely and sad. He met children who were hungry and poor. He invited them to church so they could hear about Jesus and get food to eat. Though many years have passed since Jonathan's visit, the people he met in Botswana still love to talk about how he brightened their lives with kindness.

What makes you feel happy? Do you have a favorite thing to do? Or a favorite place to go?

This extraordinary boy may have loved adventure and airplane rides, but even more, Jonathan loved PEOPLE! He loved to laugh with his friends, and he loved to make *new* friends. His big smile could cheer anyone up, and he gave the biggest and best hugs. He *always* loved to help people! Sometimes he would carry their groceries or rake their leaves.

His heart of kindness was as big as the ocean. He gave the world something very, very special. He sprinkled sparkles of kindness everywhere he went!

World-brighteners sprinkle sparkles of kindness. That is what they do!
You can be a world-brightener too!

Helping his mommy and daddy was *very* important to Jonathan! **VROOM!** He loved to vacuum the house, take out the trash, and pick up his toys. His face would light up with a huge smile, and he'd say to his mommy, "I'm a big-time helper!"

One day, he noticed a broken railing on their front porch. Because it was damaged, he thought he could "help" by using a hammer to remove ALL the railings on the entire front porch! *CRASH! BANG!* The porch looked like it had been hit by a tornado! He thought he had "fixed" it and proudly showed his parents. They were patient and kind. His daddy was as cool as a cucumber. His mommy's eyes were big and round like pepperoni pizzas! "Whoopsie," sighed his mommy. And his daddy said, "It's okay. Everybody makes mistakes."

Jonathan also loved being a "big-time" helper in the kitchen! He would sweep the floor and load the dishwasher. But sometimes, he accidentally broke a glass or dish. His parents knew he was trying his best, and they were patient and kind. "Whoopsie," sighed his mommy. And his daddy said, "It's okay. Everybody makes mistakes."

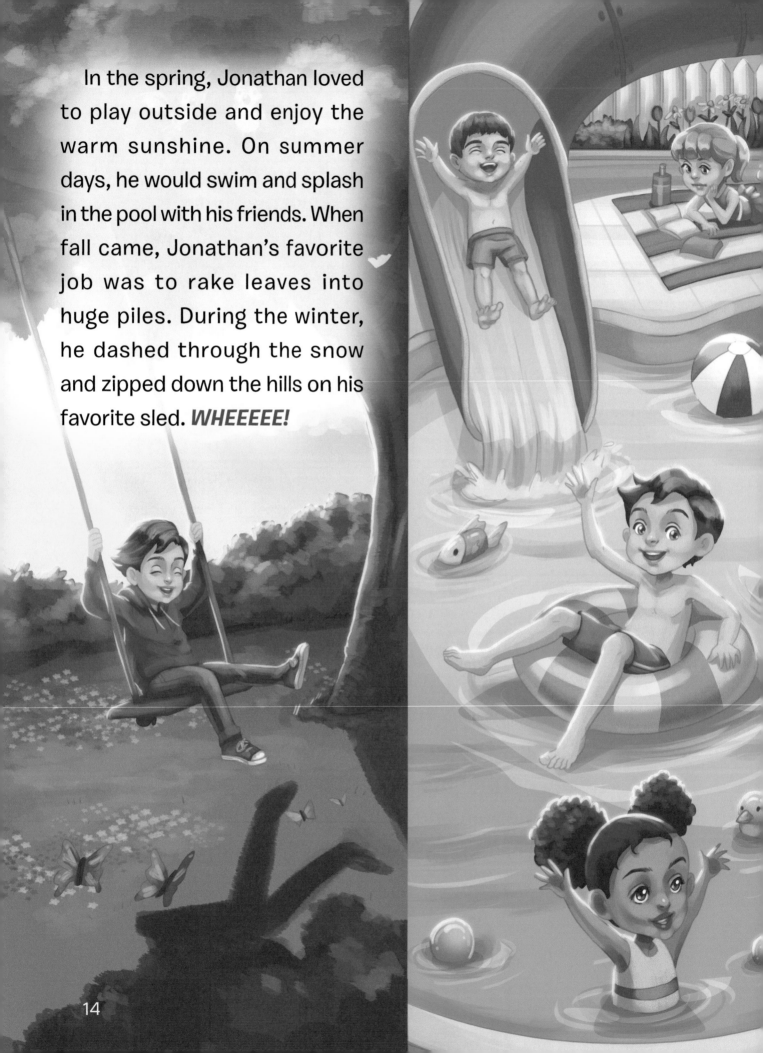

In the spring, Jonathan loved to play outside and enjoy the warm sunshine. On summer days, he would swim and splash in the pool with his friends. When fall came, Jonathan's favorite job was to rake leaves into huge piles. During the winter, he dashed through the snow and zipped down the hills on his favorite sled. **WHEEEEE!**

One blustery winter day, Jonathan looked out his window to see that snow had covered everything like a fluffy, white blanket. He quickly bundled up in his snowsuit to shovel the sidewalk. Next, he brushed the thick snow off his dad's new car. However, he mistakenly used a *shovel* instead of a *brush*. **SCREECH!** Now the car was covered with *long* scratches from the shovel! But, his parents were patient and kind. "Whoopsie," sighed his mommy. And his daddy said, "It's okay. Everybody makes mistakes."

Even world-brighteners make mistakes.
They say, "Sorry!" when they do!
You can be a world-brightener too!

The day Jonathan attended a recital is a day that will never be forgotten. Jonathan sat on the edge of his seat, waiting to hear the soloist sing her recital song. Although she had practiced and practiced... she was so nervous that her voice just wasn't cooperating *at all*. She felt as if she had butterflies in her stomach and a frog stuck in her throat. As Jonathan watched, he felt sad for her. Then, suddenly, with a *THUD* and a *THUMP*, he jumped on the stage! "Can I help you?" asked Jonathan. The crowd was stunned! And the little girl was stunned, too! As a matter of fact, she was so surprised she forgot all about being nervous and began to sing her song *beautifully! "HOORAY!"* cheered the crowd. The girl smiled. And Jonathan smiled back.

World-brighteners sprinkle sparkles of kindness by helping people! That is what they do! You can be a world-brightener too!

If we could take Jonathan's acts of kindness and wrap them in gift boxes, we would be wrapping and wrapping and wrapping.... *CRINKLE! CRINKLE! SNIP! SNIP!* And we would need an ENORMOUS amount of ribbon!

18

Just imagine! We would have so many gifts of kindness that they would fill a super-duper, extra long, GIGANTIC bridge! It didn't matter if people were tall or short. It didn't matter if they were old or young. It didn't matter if they were big or little. Jonathan would sprinkle sparkles of kindness wherever he went!

Jonathan's kindness touched thousands of people all around the world. He now lives in heaven with Jesus. Even though his friends and family miss him very much, they will never forget his big smile, huge hugs, and kind heart. They will always remember Jonathan was **extraordinary**...because he was **kind**. He inspired people around him to choose kindness, too.

There could **never** be anyone more kind than God...because God is love! He showed us His love by sending His Son, Jesus, to save us from our sins. When we believe in Jesus, He invites us to live in heaven with Him someday! Jesus changed the world with His kindness. And, as God's children, He wants us to change our world with kindness! In Ephesians 2:10, God tells us He created us to do *amazing* things. Just like fireworks light up the night sky, we can light up our world with kindness. When you choose to be kind, you could change someone's day...***you could even change someone's life!***

*World-brighteners inspire others to be kind!
That is what they do! You can be
a world-brightener too!*

Wouldn't it be exciting if somebody wrote a book about *YOU* someday? Would it be full of stories about you sprinkling sparkles of kindness? The Bible says, "If you try to be kind and good, you will be blessed with *life* and *goodness* and *honor*." (CEV) God has an incredible story to write with *your* life! He has a perfect plan—***just for you!***

When you choose kindness...everyone wins! You'll brighten someone's day, *and you'll feel better too!!* And that's like frosting on top of a cupcake!

Maybe you'd like to be a great basketball player or graceful gymnast someday...you will need to practice! Kindness takes practice, too! Each time you are kind, it makes it easier to be kind the next time...and the next time! *With your kindness, you'll become a world-brightener!*

Shine bright and sprinkle a sparkle of kindness TODAY!

Can you find the world-brighteners who are giving gifts of kindness?

All About Jonathan

Mom and Jonathan at 1 year old

Jonathan at 2 years old

Aunt Mary and Jonathan at 3 years old

"I'm being a good boy. I'm making pies like Aunt Mary!" said Jonathan.

Jonathan with his brothers Joshua & David

Jonathan on a rollercoaster with his brother, David

Jonathan in Botswana

Jonathan walking Grandma down the aisle at Uncle Scott and Aunt Mary's wedding

Dad with Jonathan on his bike

Jonathan and cousin Elizabeth

Jonathan and Dad

Jonathan and Mom

Jonathan and Aunt Mary shopping on his 33rd birthday

More About Jonathan

Jonathan was diagnosed with a brain-based genetic disorder when he was 3 years old. He lived with his loving and devoted parents until heaven welcomed him home at 33 years old. His cheerfulness was inspiring, his laugh was contagious, and his smile would light up the room.

Jonathan's heart was full of love for Jesus. He loved attending church, having devotions, singing worship songs, and preaching to everyone who would listen. His parents purchased a pulpit for his "home sermons." His mom helped him memorize almost 50 Bible verses, and he integrated those into his "sermons." (Yes, his dad and mom were over-the-top amazing parents!)

Jonathan *was never too busy or too tired to spend time with Jesus.* If you visited his home, you'd probably hear him singing worship songs, playing his tambourine, or preaching a sermon. He probably would've invited you to stay for dinner, too!

Taking a trip to the grocery store or Taco Bell was always exciting for him! If you were in Jonathan's line of sight, he would find a way to greet you with a big hello and a bright smile. One of his favorite greetings was "Major Hellos!"

Jonathan's legacy of kindness will never be forgotten.

About the Author

Mary Demoff is married to a wonderful husband, Scott. Together they have four incredibly amazing teenagers and an adorable dog.

Mary is a blogger, teacher, ministry coordinator, and speaker. She loves spending time with her family, organizing parties and events, and volunteering as a Junior Bible Quiz coordinator and coach.

As Jonathan's aunt, Mary was privileged to play a big part in his life and would invite him to spend weekends with her and her family. She loved him dearly and believes his life can continue to positively impact our world today.

People desperately need to see God's kindness through His people. Mary's tribute to Jonathan is a story she couldn't keep from sharing so that his sparkles of kindness would continue to brighten our world.

Printed in the United States
by Baker & Taylor Publisher Services